Dropshipping

A Beginners Guide to Making Money Within 30 Days (2020 Edition)

by Marcus Pereira

Table of Contents

What Will This Book Teach You?

If you are planning on becoming an e-commerce entrepreneur, specifically in the art of dropshipping, then this book is for you as you will see many benefits. The beauty of dropshipping is that you don't need to keep actual stock or inventory of the items you want to sell. In this book, we will look at all the beginner information you would need to kick start your first every dropshipping business.

You will be filled in with the details on how to start a dropshipping store and most importantly, how to keep it. Dropshipping is among the easiest and profitable businesses in the e-commerce world especially for those without a huge capital to work and run with, but they are still interested to sell and make money.

This book gives a comprehensive guide on what dropshipping is, a good introduction as well as who is it for, who it isn't for and the pros and cons. You will also learn the how to select a niche, the various methods involved in dropshipping as well as risks or common mistakes in dropshipping.

You will also be guided on finding the right suppliers in your business because suppliers are the backbone of any dropshipping site.

Introduction

Every day, the thought of running your own online business becomes more vivid and pronounced. Every day, you work on getting this dream a reality whether it is reading about doing your own business, saving up money, talking to people or finding your niche - you are making small progress and then one day, you just do it. You open your laptop, you sign up for a platform and you're establishing the foundations of your dream.

The reality is, with the internet and using the dropship business model, setting up and running your own online business is easier compared to setting up a brick-and-stone store. With a few simple clicks, you are already on your way in setting up an e-commerce site and actively investing in your success.

What is Dropshipping?

Dropshipping is an element of retail fulfillment practice in the standard retail model that allows a store selling products and merchandise to not hold its own inventory or, in other words, do away with keeping their products in stock, or shipping their products to their customers on their own or owning a warehouse to store its products.

In this case, whenever there is an order for the product, the seller purchases its item from a third-party vendor and this third-party vendor ships it directly to the customer. This retailer partner with a dropship supplier that does the manufacturing, warehousing, packaging, and shipping of these products, on the retailer's behalf. The merchant does not see or handles the said product.

Chapter 1 - Pros & Cons of Dropshipping

Dropshipping is different from the other retails models due to this major factor - the retail owner or merchant does not own inventory or stock. The merchant instead purchases this inventory as and when it is needed from their third-party supplier that focuses on manufacturing or wholesaling, in order to meet customer demands.

In other words, dropshipping works as below:

- The customer makes an order for a product seen on the merchant's online store.

- The merchant records the order purchase and automatically sends this to the dropship supplier, complete with order details and customer information.

- The dropship supplier packages the product and ships it according to the customer's given information.

This is an extremely effective and attractive business model as it eliminates the purpose of the merchant to have a physical business venue like an office space or even a warehouse. All they ever need is internet access, a website and a device connected to the internet to upload, update and store information on their products and services if any.

Pros of Dropshipping

There are plenty of benefits to this dropshipping business model. These are:

- It is extremely easy to set up. Unlike setting up a brick-and-mortar business space, this retail model only involves just three steps which is i) finding the supplier ii) setting up a good website and once that is done iii) selling your products and services

- This model is easy to understand and implement especially for a new coming into the e-commerce industry

- To set up your business with the dropship model, the cost involved is literally next to nothing. Unlike in traditional business models where the major costs go into the setting and running of the operations, in dropshipping this step is eliminated and all the cost you need to think of is the applications you need to run your website, domain registration, hosting as well as themes you use - which is not much.

- There are no unreasonably high overhead costs involved. The merchant or business owner can do away with renting or buying warehouses to store their products and also do away with utility bills that come with it. The costs of managing the website are all they need to worry about.

- Dropshipping risks are significantly lower because there is little to no pressure about selling inventory.

- This type of business model can be run from anywhere meaning the business owner or merchant's location independent. There is no warehouse, no sales location, no offices, not much employees and no hassles.

- There is little to absolutely no commitment to a physical space requirement which means the business owner can run their business by the beach, in their home, while flying on the plane. All you need is an internet connection and your laptop, iPad, tablet or any device you can access the internet with.

- You can sell just about anything over the internet and there's a dropship supplier for almost anything out there. Either sell only one product, or a mix of products - it is entirely up to you. Just find your niche and the right dropship supplier you need.

- You will have more time and resources to look into scaling your business. With traditional business models, the more you profit, the more work you have to put in and the more you need to invest in the resource section. Of course, even with the dropshipping model, you need to put in some investment but not to a huge amount. Dropshipping enables you to send more orders to your supplier, from here on you let them handle everything else while all you need to do is earn profits.

- Dropshipping also reduces losses on damaged goods. Shipment is directly from supplier to customer and because there are fewer shipment steps involved, the risk of the items being damaged is also reduced.

Cons of Dropshipping

Where there are pros, there are also cons even when it comes to dropshipping. Here are some of them:

- You will receive slightly lower profit margins compared to sourcing from a manufacturer or a wholesaler. Dropship suppliers will charge you higher prices depending on your niche, requirements, and location and this will cut into your profit margins.

- You must bear complete liability if anything goes wrong, even if it is the supplier's fault. The customer purchases the product from your site- the merchant's website. In the event, something happens or if the supplier doesn't keep their end of the bargain or messes up, it is still the merchant's fault. Your customers will contact you because you are the face of the brand. Therefore, it is extremely important to hire the right dropship supplier.

- You have lower control over the creative process. Your customers will have lesser satisfaction with your product because you will not be able to determine personalized packaging or the branding of the shipped products- this is dependent on the supplier.

- You have less control over how your product is presented during the fulfillment and delivery process as this is the supplier's job to ship the products to the customers. However, having the right supplier and establishing a good relationship with them will give you better control as some suppliers will go the extra mile in ensuring your creative process is delivered through the product. However, this may cost more.

- There may be more issues especially when it comes to shipping. Selling multiple products is a good idea as it can increase sales and make you profit, however, it can also pose a problem if the merchant has too many suppliers to deal with for each product they sell. Also, different suppliers will change different shipping costs as this would depend on where they are located and what kind of product you have.

- The competition in dropshipping retail is extremely high due to the attractiveness and the popularity of this business model. Unless the merchant caters to an extremely specific niche, the competition is detrimental.

- It is hard to keep track of the inventory from the supplier. Due to miscommunications due to cancellations and having backorders. However, with new software coming in and improved communication abilities, this matter can be solved. Of course, this software also comes with a price and may also increase your overhead costs.

How Viable and Profitable is Dropshipping?

Profit margins for dropshipping usually range from 15% to 45%. For consumer goods such as luxury items and durables, the profit margin can be up to 100%. When it comes to dropshipping, it entirely depends on the kind of niche you are in and then getting the right supplier. You do not want to enter a heavily saturated market.

One of the better ways to ensure higher margins is to source directly from the manufacturer and not the vendor/supplier. This cuts out the middleman. Once the business gains traction, it can become an effective money-making means that it only involves little input. To potential to earn up to one million dollars is real, although not for every dropshipping business.

Who is Dropshipping for?

If you are a first timer entering the online business, then dropshipping is a great business model, to begin with. It is low-risk and low-investment which is great for novices starting their own business. It does not involve much monetary gamble.

It is ideal for someone who is a current owner of a retail store and already has an inventory, but looking to reach newer, wider markets. This business model, however, does not give you amazing results from the get-go. Dropshipping margins are relatively lower so this might not bode well for a startup brand because these businesses do not have ultimate control where customer satisfaction, related to brand experience and branding is concerned.

Here Are the Types of Entrepreneurs Dropshipping Will Benefit:

- **The Validating Entrepreneur**

  Dropshipping is a great way to test new products or even new startup products before an entrepreneur can begin heavily ingesting into the inventory required to sell. This makes it the perfect business model for entrepreneurs that require high levels of product validation before they begin investing heavily.

- **The Budget Entrepreneur**

  Dropship qualifies as the least expensive business model for online selling because you do not need to purchase inventory upfront. Due to this, the dropshipping method sells effectively for entrepreneurs that are on a budget or are looking to keep startup costs low.

- **The First Time Entrepreneur**

  Selling online is not as easy as it seems to be so for the first-time online entrepreneur, the dropshipping method works well. Understanding how to market the product online and drive and convert traffic takes time to figure out as well as optimize. Dropshipping allows online entrepreneurs to learn the ropes of online commerce, conversion and driving traffic before they begin investing thousands in an inventory.

- **The Multi-Variety Entrepreneur**

Dropshipping is an ideal model to use for retailers who want to sell a variety of products simple for the reason that you do not need to purchase inventory upfront.

Who Isn't Dropshipping for?

- **The Brand Centric Entrepreneur**

Building a brand around a product is difficult but the rewards are long-term and worthwhile. However, it is exponentially difficult to build a brand using the dropshipping retail method because there are plenty of other elements connected to the entire customer experience that the brand-centric entrepreneur will not be part of.

For instance, there will be times when a customer has made a purchase for a product. You, the merchant finds it's sold out with the dropship supplier. This is not only inconvenient for you as the merchant but also frustrating to the customer. It is even more frustrating to coordinate between dropshipper and customer to determine a solution. Since you are not shipping the product on your own, you also do not have control of the packaging which is an extension of the brand experience.

While some merchants are okay with that, asking yourself if this bothers you will help determine if dropshipping is for you. You also will not be able to create a relationship with shipping companies because you do not do the shipping. When something goes wrong in the shipping process, coordinating with the shipping companies can prove to be difficult. You need to coordinate with the shipping account representative, who is already busy, and this might take a few days to sort out.

- **The Margin Focused Entrepreneur**

One of the biggest problems with dropshipping is its thin margin lines. Gross margins for traditional dropshipping products is around 10 to 20%. After you pay off your credit card transaction fees, e-commerce fees, and other online services, you are looking at only a small percent of your margin left. While there are online entrepreneurs who earn big, up to a million dollars of revenue each year, their profit margins are around 40k to 50k once all these fees are deducted.

- **The Non-Creative Marketer**

With more manufacturers, chances are they're also dropshippers of their own products and they also have the same exact goals in sales which are about 30% coming from direct-to-consumer sales and this is usually from their own e-commerce site. This would mean that to sell their product, you are competing directly with your own supplier. This supplier has many other advantages such as higher margins than you on the same existing product.

Competing with them head-to-head is a waste of time and resource because most of the time, they win out all because they can afford to. You need to be creative and exploit other channels that they are not using to acquire the same target market and beat them. Relying on Google Adwords or Facebook Ads isn't going to cut it.

Chapter 2 - Finding your Niche in Dropshipping

Finding your Niche in Dropshipping

It may sound overwhelming to find your niche in business because there are plenty of things that you can get involved in. While it does sound overwhelming, it is not hard as there are a few methods that you can employ to find that perfect niche that would give you profits. Here are some methods that you may want to try in looking for the right niche:

Tip #1 - Brainstorming

Brainstorming is always effective for practically anything you need to work on- ideas, solutions, methods and finding the right niche. To begin brainstorming ideas for your niches, meet up with your business partner or like-minded friends who will be able to help you or someone you trust. Friends and family who know you and your business partner are the most ideal. Next, you want to block off time to focus on your brainstorming - so set a meeting, time and date for this.

When you meet, one of the things to think about is the items that you, your business partner or friends have bought online or recently purchased. Write these things down, even if it perplexes you. There will be tons of niches that are profitable but that does not mean you should rush into the business of dropshipping. When you have your niches, list them down and filter them according to:

- Competition: Look out for other dropshipping stores and investigate the kinds of products that are oversaturated. You do not want to get into selling these.

- Loyalty: Avoid getting into niches that are dominated by national brand

- Pricing: The higher the price of the product, the higher the margin profits

- Weight: The winning combo is a high-priced product, but it has low shipping weights.

- Returns: Do not go for products that have different sizes and style preferences - they usually come with high return rates

Tip #2 - Research, Compare and Evaluate Dropshipping Trends

eBay is one of the places to check whether items sell online but do not use eBay to determine the price of your products as eBay's prices are relatively low.

Once you get onto eBay, one of the things you want to research is to identify the products in the different niches in the higher-priced bracket, the ones that are expensive, so it can be anything like $50 or $200 or $500 depending on the product.

When you get your search results, allow it to show 'completed listings'. Completed lists shows items in red or green, red being the item did not sell and green is sold.

Look at the items only for the products you are considering to niche in - it is okay to go over this list a few times until you identify about 20 products within your niche that sells out almost always - at least 10 units a day.

From here, request for price lists from various suppliers, get shipping quotes from customs brokers as well as storage capacities for a product.

Tip #3 - Utilize Amazon

Being the world's largest retailer, Amazon sells everything imaginable.

Because of this, Amazon is one of the best things on the Internet to find profitable niches and other amazing possibilities that you never thought of.

Here's how you can find red hot profitable niches using Amazon:

- First, click on the 'All' tab located on the left side of the main search bar. You will see niches or a list of categories

- Click on a category that interests you and clicks on 'Go'.

- When the new page pops up, you will see on the left, a list of 'sub-niches'.

- By clicking on a subcategory, you will then see more specific sub-niches.

- You now have specific niches! You can go down this list if you really want to.

Amazon is also a great place to help you in a specific niche as well as the product that sells the best.

You can also choose 'best sellers' from the navigation bar located just right under the search bar at the top of the page. You can see all the items that are currently selling the best.

Tip #4 - Put on Your Marketing Cap

One of the best things you can sell with dropshipping is to sell EXPENSIVE items.

The average dropshipping profit is about 20% of your total sales. You make 20% profit on an item that is $1,000 which is $200 or 20% on an item that is $10 which makes you $2.

If you want to start making money, start selling the big toys. Sounds simple but in truth, you need to do more research.

You also need to identify potential future competition, which are other online retailers who are selling the items you want to sell.

The roadblock here is there is no way to find out how much money a retailer makes on each sale at this point unless you use a MAP procedure.

Should I Choose Passion or Money in a Niche?

It really depends on you. To some people, starting a business in dropshipping also means that they can work on a product or be doing business that they love.

Where as to some, they find motivation the more money they see in their bank account and they don't care what they sell.

The truth is, you want to make a profit for any kind of venture or business you are in. So, you will most likely investigate a balancing act of pursuing your passion and creating a successful profit line.

Having said that, you still need to have interest into the product that you are selling because it will keep you motivated to explore even further on your audience needs which will also help you align your content. When it comes to pursuing your passion, it doesn't necessarily mean that you'd be successful.

So How So We Balance the Two?

Passion does lead the way. Finding profitable niches to things, items and products that you are passionate about not only makes your bank account healthy but also it makes you have fun and love what you do.

To help you discover your passion, if you already have not, let's look at niches that are based on your passions. Here are some questions you can ask:

- What kind of blogs and websites do you interact with and visit the most?

- What kind of pages or accounts do you follow on social media that you enjoy?

- Which online stores do you usually purchase from?

- What do you think are your biggest obsessions?

- What kind of products do you usually collect or buy most frequently?

- If you had $1000 to spend on any product you *want* (not need), what would you buy?

Now answer these questions to create a shortlist based on your passions.

Next, if you want to choose a niche based on how much money you can make, then you might want to ask yourself these set of questions:

- Which online retailers have been increasing in popularity lately and what products do they sell? (Answer these questions focusing on a few specific niche-based retailers instead of big names like Amazon)

- Which products are the most popular right now?

- Which products have the highest profit margin?

- Which niches hold the biggest audiences?

Evergreen Niches vs Trending Niches

An evergreen niche is a niche that most retailers would like - it stands the test of time. Things like gaming, beauty, and fashion and weight loss are very evergreen niches. However, on the other hand, trending niches have instant profits and surge, but it also falls in popularity fast.

Tools that you can use for finding a Niche Market

There are a variety of different tools that you can use to create shortlists of niche ideas in order to determine if you can see any niches that show signs of being highly profitable or aligned within your passions.

First, start your search with these:

- Oberlo

- Amazon

- AliExpress

- Treadhunter

On all these websites, you can easily find the trending niches. Keep your eye out for niches that keep coming up and also try to find potential sub-niches that you find interesting that would complement each other.

Trending Products Blog Posts

Another thing to look out for is updated product lists. Oberlo is a company that regularly shares updated product lists to ensure that they are always at the forefront of today's most popular products.

These lists can also help you determine what you want to niche on. Apart from that, keep an eye out for blog posts with lists such as:

- 20 of the best gardening tools to have in 2018

- 30 Fail-proof Business ideas to make money in 2018

- Best Buy Beauty Products for Summer 2018

- Top 10 Polishes to Get your Car Shining like Brand new

Check out the products that these articles mention as well as the dropshipping products being sold and the business ideas related to it.

Wikipedia's List of Hobbies

Wikipedia's list of hobbies is a great way to find a niche of practically anything that you can think of from hobbies to passion, from crocheting to baton twirling, resin art to golfing, furniture restoration and terrariums - you will be surprised to find an extremely extensive list of both indoor and outdoor hobbies. Look into the lists if there are any hobbies that compliment your passions or investigate researching to see find profitable niches that are within these categories. Some hobbies are popular enough to have a large market of followers, so you can build an entire store dedicated to selling these products or the items that help these hobbyist work on their passions.

The amazing thing about hobbies is that you will like-minded people join groups and spend the money to pursue their hobbies. This itself gains you an audience you can immediately sell to. Some of the hobbies on the list that you can build e-commerce stores for include:

- Jewelry making

- Astrology

- Do it yourself

- Fashion

- Flower arranging

- Gardening

- Magic

- Pet

- Various fitness niches

- Baking

Google Trends

Yes, Google Trends is another tool you can use to discover your niche. What you want to look out for are niches that have a stable growth, no matter how slight.

Do you need to be an expert in finding your niche?

You do not necessarily need to be a niche expert, but some experience will help. It may be slightly harder to build a successful brand without having some kind of niche experience although it is not entirely impossible.

Alternatively, you can also fake it till you make it. This means that you can just find the right target audience through Facebook ads as well. You can also engage influencers using the power of Instagram to build an audience as this can lead to sales.

Having some idea about the niche you are getting into will also help you create content that resonates with your audience. No experience may render it harder to reach them and bring that traffic to your store.

On the other hand, you can also outsource these blog writing tasks to ghostwriters or someone equivalent. But most entrepreneurs do this, especially when starting out to keep costs slow.

As mentioned previously, getting into selling a product you somewhat like and having some expertise in the niche can help motivate you, in the long run, to sustain your business, especially if the money isn't hitting the profit margins like you want to.

FB Search

Another tool you can use is FB search and this tool can help you determine the amount of engagement your posts get. You can also use this as a competitor analysis tool, so you can see the posts of both your competitors, as well as customers, make. You can also look up at the brands that are within your niche.

Search using specific keywords to search. Your search will turn up based on people, pages, photos, videos, links, and marketplace. When you look at these pages, you can see the number of followers. It will also help you understand the kind of frequency your Facebook posts need to be, which is somewhere between 1-2 posts per day to have a competitive advantage and scale quickly.

Browsing the pages that come up in your search also gives you an idea of the direction of your marketing strategy, looking through photos helps you understand the kind of material you need to create and the markets you can target.

Continue your research

Here are several other things to look at before you start building your store. You want to make sure that you have an audience for your niche even before you were spending hours on marketing your website and buying ads online.

Here's a quick list of what to look for:

- What kind of social platforms do people market your niche?

- Are there dedicated Facebook groups for your niche?

- Are there targeting options you can use on Facebook for this niche?

- What kind of forums exists for people to discuss the niche?

- Do people host events for this niche?

- Do influencers post about this niche?

- Are there fans for your niche?

Pinterest, YouTube, Instagram and of course Facebook are all popular places to look if your niches are talked about on these platforms. It is always better to put your content where it is seen, heard and spoken because there is where your audience spends time on.

Another thing is, all these platforms have one element in common. They are all heavy on visuals which means, stunning images and video reach out to your audience faster.

Chapter 3 - Looking for and Choosing your Suppliers

There are many important elements that you need to think about when choosing your dropship suppliers. In this chapter, we will explore how to find one, how to differentiate between a supplier and a retailer and legal matters.

Finding Wholesale Suppliers

There are several strategies that you can use to find wholesale suppliers, some being effective and some now. There is a list of methods that you can try, starting with the most effective.

Contact the Manufacturer

Contacting the direct source is one of the best ways. Once you know the product you are planning on selling, pick up the phone and call the manufacturer who focuses on this product and asks for a list of their wholesale distributes.

Contact these wholesalers and inquire about opening an account with them. In doing so, you will be able to source a selection of products more efficiently and easily in the niche that you want.

Try Oberlo

Through Oberlo, you will be able to easily import products from suppliers to your online store and if you want, you can also ship directly to your customers – all in just a few clicks. Using Oberlo, you can fulfill orders automatically, do product customization as well as pricing automation.

Google It!

It may seem like a pronounced solution. However, there are rules that you should follow when using Google:

- You must conduct an extensive search - while you most likely will have thousands of results for wholesalers, you may not find the top ten on your search results because wholesalers are not very good in both marketing or promoting their business.

- Don't judge the website by its front page - most wholesalers websites are outdated. Refer to point above. While some wholesalers do put to get a good website out, don't get let down by a poorly design site.

- Use modifiers - when searching on Google, use other kinds of keywords such as 'reseller' or 'bulk' or 'warehouse'.

Order from the Competition

This may be one way to locate a supplier - by making a small order with an opposing company. When you receive your package, use Google to find the return address to find out the original shipper.

You can also contact the supplier to find out. This is not a method to rely on, but a good solution nonetheless.

Attend Trade Shows

Attending trade shows allows you to meet and network with manufacturers and wholesalers in the niche that you want to retail in.

This method works great only if you have picked your niche and the product that you want to sell within that niche.

Invest a little bit of time attending these shows - meeting your suppliers and manufacturers face to face helps build business partnerships.

Directories

A directory is supplier database which is another way of scoring a good selection of suppliers based on market or niche. Many directories use a screening process to legitimize their suppliers and ensure they try are genuine wholesalers. While these lists are beneficial, they are not something you need.

Finding major suppliers can be done with a little bit of digging especially when you've established the product or niche you won't sell.

This is a nice to have, not a must-have. Supplier directory is a convenient method to search quickly and browse many suppliers.

Before You Contact Suppliers

So now that you have a solid list of suppliers, it's time to move on to the next step - contacting them. Before you do that, get yourself equipped using these guidelines:

- **You Need to Be Legal** – legitimate wholesalers will need proof of your business even before you can open an account with them. Pricing is only revealed once a customer has been approved so apart from making sure your wholesale is legal, you also need to be legally incorporated, so you have the right documents and licenses.

- **Understand How You Appear** – having a great business plan just won't cut it with wholesale suppliers as they often get these from retailers, accompanied with questions that take up their time but, in the end, no order is made. Be aware that suppliers are not going to empathize with you.

  While they are happy to help set you up with a dropshipping account, don't expect them to give you discounts or even spend hours on the phone or on email with you.

  You need to make a purchase first because otherwise, you will earn a bad reputation which can spread quickly and hurt your relationship with other potential suppliers.

- Build credibility first before even attempting to make special requests and be definite about your business plans such as launch dates, shipping dates, and quantities instead of giving vague ideas. You also want to communicate your professional successes in the past because it can help with your dealings with a supplier. Your objective is to convince suppliers that dealing with you - despite your special requests - will pay off when you become successful and start bringing in more business.

- **A tele-conversation helps** – While many are more confident about sending emails, picking up the phone and making a call is a better prospect of securing a partnership with your supplier. Some issues just need to be tended on the phone as opposed to emails.

  You can send follow up emails after a tele-conversation. Suppliers always have people calling them, including people new to the business. More often than not, you'll get a sales representative that is more than happy to answer your questions.

If you are planning to call a supplier, a good tip would be to write the questions you want to ask them. It will be easier to make this call when you have your questions to ask.

How to Find Good Suppliers

In the world of dropshipping, it is important to work with the right supplier especially since suppliers are a crucial element of this entire dropshipping process. Like everything in life, dropshipping suppliers also come in different sizes, needs, and interest.

In finding the right kind of suppliers, here are some attributes you want to look out for:

- **They Have Professional Staff and Targeted to the Industry**

  Suppliers who are professional also have a sales rep that is equipped with the knowledge of industry needs and they are also trained with the know-how of the industry and the product lines that they are dealing with.

  If you are in a niche product line, calling these sales reps and getting their invaluable insight is an asset to your dropshipping business, especially if you're not overly familiar with either.

- **They Have Dedicated Support Representatives**

  Most of the time when you contact a good quality supplier, you will usually be assigned to an individual sales representative who will not only deal with the issues you have but also ensure that they are every step of the way with you from the introduction, product information, make a sale and sometimes even after-sales.

Suppliers who do not assign specific sales representatives often give you more problems because issues take longer to resolve, and you usually have to end up calling them until the issue is resolved. Having a single supplier contact who deals exclusively with your case for solving your issues is really important and crucial.

- **They are Invested in Technology**

We did say that suppliers usually do not have updated websites. While this should not be a cause for you to reject them, quality suppliers do understand the benefits of having a well-functioning website. Most of the time, they are also easier to work with.

Suppliers who provide a comprehensive product catalog online and searchable order history make your life easy too. So while wholesalers are not really tech savvy, to begin with, engaging with one that does place importance in a good website helps in the long run.

- **They Can Take Orders via Email**

Having to make a call or manually place orders on the website is a tedious task, not only is it time intensive, it is also cutting back on your resources. When choosing your supplier, find one that makes ordering through email a seamless process.

- **They are Centrally Located**

A centrally located supplier is beneficial no matter where you are. Location is imperative and a supplier that is conveniently located enable packages to be shipped and delivered within 2 to 3 business days. Suppliers located at coastal areas often take a week or more to get orders shipped and delivered.

Conveniently located suppliers also allow you to consistently promote your customers faster delivery times, enabling you to save more money on fees and having a happy customer.

- **They are Organized and Efficient**

  Having competent staff and excellent systems is like having a well-tuned and functional website. It reduces errors, saves time and keeps both parties happy.

  Incompetent staff results in false orders and unhappy customers. The issue here is difficult to know how competent a supplier is without using it, which is why reading reviews are important.

Another way to identify good suppliers is to place small orders to get a sense of their processes, sales reps, and professionalism. This way, you can identify:

- How efficient their ordering process is?

- How fast items are shipped out

- How efficient are they in following up with an invoice for tracking information?

- How good is the quality of their packing?

Your Options on Paying Suppliers

Suppliers usually accept payments in these two ways:

- **Credit Card**

  Credit card payment is usually the preferred payment for suppliers especially if you are new and establishing a presence in the industry.

  Once you have a thriving business, credit cards are still the best option as they are more convenient especially for making online payments. You get points on your card whenever you make frequent payments too.

  You can also obtain a higher volume of purchases via your credit card minus having to deal with the actual out-of-pocket expense.

- **Net Terms**

  Net terms on an invoice is another common way to pay suppliers. When using this method, you are usually given a certain period to pay off the supplier.

  For example, if you have a "net 30" terms, this means you have exactly 30 days from the purchase date to pay your supplier. You can do this either by check or a bank draw.

You would also need to provide credit references by the supplier before they allow your net payment terms because this means you are lending money from them.

This is common in the dropshipping or e-commerce industry so don't worry if you are asked to provide documentation when you use net terms to pay.

How to Spot Fake Dropshipping Wholesalers

In a world of good suppliers, you will also come across fake and bad suppliers. Unfortunately, wholesalers who are legitimate are usually bad at marketing which makes it harder to find them.

This usually means that you will find wholesalers that are not genuine. They are usually middle persons who end up in your search results because they are better marketers. You need to be more cautious if this.

The following methods will help you differentiate whether a wholesale supplier is legitimate or fake:

- You are asked for monthly fees – If you are engaging a genuine wholesale, they will not impose a fee just to do business with them.

  If a supplier asks for a monthly membership or service fee, this is a huge red light. That said, you should also learn to differentiate between supplier directories and suppliers.

Supplier directories list wholesale suppliers and they are usually efficiently organized by product types or market and go through a screening process to ensure the suppliers are legitimate.

These directories will charge a fee to keep these suppliers on their list and for website maintenance. This shouldn't be taken as a sign the directory itself is illegitimate.

- Their business is not entirely wholesale – To procure genuine wholesale pricing you must apply for a wholesale account because this proves that you are indeed a legitimate business. You need to be approved before you can place your first order.

  Wholesale suppliers that offer products to the public at "wholesale prices" are just a retailer offering items at inflated prices.

While monthly fees are usually a red flag sign, there are some dropshipping fees which are legitimate. Here are some of them:

- **Pre-Order Fees** – Plenty of dropship suppliers charge a shipping fee that ranges from $2 to $5 depending on the items that they are to ship - the size and complexity will usually determine these prizes.

This is standard practice in the industry because the shipping and packing costs for individual products are higher than if they were bulk orders.

- **Minimum Order** - You will need to place a minimum order which is usually at the lowest amount if this is your first order. This is done to filter out merchants who are only there to window shop and this also lessens time in answering questions that do not translate to meaningful businesses.

This could cause issues if you are dropshipping. If you feel that ordering a pre-order amount is too risky, you can also offer to pre-pay your supplier that applies with your shipping orders.

This way you are building credit with them and it allows you to meet the supplier's minimum requirement but also prevents you from placing a large single order without any initial orders made by your customers on your site.

Chapter 4 - Setting Up Your Dropshipping Business

Dropshipping, thanks to advancements on the internet, is an extremely popular business. The internet makes marketing capacities outweigh financial needs.

One of the biggest pull factors is that you do not need stock or even to handle the things that you are selling, and you can also start with limited funds.

In its very basic idea, dropshipping requires a website optimized for e-commerce. You purchase items from a third-party supplier who then fulfills an order made by a customer on your e-commerce website.

This cuts operational costs and frees up your time to focus on other aspects of the business such as customer acquisition - marketing and promoting your website.

Want to start your own dropshipping business? Here are some fundamental steps to follow:

Ideally, it doesn't take a lot to start a dropshipping business, neither do you need huge startup funds to launch your business.

Once you launch it, you will need to work hard to ensure that your business is sustainable and gives you the profit you desire.

1. Start by Selecting a Niche

We covered this in the previous chapter. As mentioned, the niche you select must be something that you have some interest in as well as knowledge in. This is what will keep you going and will make it easier for you to market it.

Without passion in the niche you select, you will be more prone to become discouraged and feel like giving up because you are not motivated. Passion will drive through to push you to level up in your dropshipping endeavors.

Here, we go through some points again to consider when selecting your niche:

- **Looking for Attractive Profits**

  Start by selling higher priced products. Selling a $30 product is essentially the same as it would be to sell a $1,300 item.

- **Low Shipping Costs are Very Important**

  While your suppliers are the ones handling the shipping, costs of shipping affect the customer experience. High shipping costs will prevent return customers from purchasing from your website.

  While you do want to concentrate on higher priced products, you want to find inexpensive shipping costs for it, because then you can possibly absorb the costs of shipping and offer your customers free shipping. This can also attract more return orders and increase sales.

- **Focus on a Product That Appeals to Impulse Buyers with Disposable Income**

You want to experience the highest conversion rate when your focus is to drive traffic to your site. This is because most visitors will never return- unless it's a product they really cannot live without.

Retaining customers are great however you also want to sell products that spark impulse purchases. You also want products that appeal to those who are financially viable to make a split-second purchasing decision.

- **Ensure That Your Product is Being Actively Searched**

At the age of the internet, keywords are extremely important as this is how customers will find. To do this, use Google's Keyword Planner and Trends to investigate keywords that people use to search your niche.

Here's where passion, interest, and knowledge into your product will be an advantage - knowing your product also means you know the search terms used.

- **Create Your Own Brand**

Increase the value of your dropshipping business by rebranding whatever it is you are selling and pass it off as your own.

- **Sell Something That Isn't Available Locally**

Look into offering a product your customer cannot get just by walking into their neighborhood store. This is another way to pick a niche.

2. Conduct a Competitive Analysis

Some of your biggest competition will come from bigger operations such as Walmart and Amazon. This doesn't mean that you should sell a product that has no competition. Produces that have no or little competition really means nobody is looking for it online or wants it.

There are of course many other reasons a product may not have competition. It could be poor profit margins, manufacturing issues, supplier issues and the biggest wreck would be the difficulty in shipping the item.

When starting your dropshipping business, start with products that have competition. Not only is it high in demand but it has a proven sustainable business track.

3. Secure the Right Supplier

Plenty of dropshipping suppliers are located overseas, specifically China. Partnering with the wrong supplier can negatively affect your business, so it's important that you do your due diligence and read the information given in Chapter 2.

Maintaining a good stream of communication with your supplier is crucial to increase the way you understand each other and communicate what your business needs.

Ask as many questions as you want and learn what their production capacities so that you are aware when your business takes off and receives more orders. Your chosen supplier needs to match your growth, so you don't need to look for one again.

4. Optimize Your Site for E-Commerce

A site optimized for e-commerce is extremely crucial in the dropshipping business model. One of the simplest platforms that you can use is Shopify as it comes with built-in, customizable apps to help you create a website, increase sales and even market your website. It is a very easy plug-and-play option.

You could also get a web design and development company to help you create an e-commerce website. However, many newbie retailers prefer using the play-and-play e-commerce, especially in the beginning.

You can then explore additional website customizations once you have a better idea of where your business is heading, have better funds and add in new approaches to your site.

5. Build a Customer Acquisition Plan

Now that you have a great product and a fantastic website, has there been any sales yet? Without customers coming to your site to purchase, you do not have any business. Announce your presence by using social media!

Depending on what you are selling, use a social media account that can best show your customers what you have to offer. Facebook, Instagram, and YouTube have the highest usage to search, explore and purchase.

You can reach out to a targeted audience easily and generate sales and revenue right from the start. This will also give you the capacity to compete with the largest brands and retailers on the get-go.

Apart from this, think ahead and start optimizing your site with search engine optimization and email marketing - allow customers who visit to opt for emailed newsletters, so you can send discounts and special offers right into their inbox.

6. Optimize and Analyze

Tracking your data, usage, and metrics enables you to understand your target audience better. Google Analytics can be used for your website and Facebook, Instagram, Twitter and YouTube all have their own analytics that you can check for data on how your customers behave for each of your posts.

You will always need to test new marketing solutions and opportunities, so you have a different social media campaign for your customers. It also helps you stay current and fresh.

Chapter 5 – Running Your Dropshipping Business

Running Your Dropshipping Business

In this chapter, you should have the fundamentals of dropshipping down pat enough to contemplate launching a business in dropshipping.

But hang on, before you start you will want to look into some really important business and financial steps if you are truly serious in getting your new venture out in the open and the very fact that you are reading this book says that you are SERIOUS about dropshipping.

Some of these procedures are a must-do while others are just good to do. However, identifying them and dealing with it now will save you time and challenges that may come ahead.

The Commitment Required

Like with any business, building a successful business in dropshipping will require your commitment and long-term perspective. However, do not set yourself up for disappointment too fast, too soon.

While you can make profits in your business, but even before you get there, you need to approach your business with a more realistic mindset and set practical expectations with regards to investment and profitability. When it comes to dropshipping, your major investments are time and money.

Investing Time

Investing your time is a much-favored approach compared to investing money from the get-go. This method is ideal for these reasons:

- Investing your time will enable you to learn how dropshipping operates inside and out. Reading books can only get you so far - it helps you start out, but it is crucial to learn the ropes on your own, so you can see your business grow and scale.

- Investing your time will help you understand and get to know target customers as well as your market, which will help you make informed decisions as your business grows.

- Investing your time also means you are less likely to spend large sums of money on 'nice-to-have' projects that are not a must-have for your business success.

- Investing your time also enables you to develop new skills that will make you a better entrepreneur as your business grows.

While you do want to quit that 9 to 5 job and spend all your time on building your dropshipping business, realistically you and most people cannot afford to do it, unless you have an investor ready to help you out or you have enough savings to help you stay afloat for at least a minimum of 6 months.

That said, it is not impossible either. You need to put some challenging time ahead, but it is possible to continue dropshipping even while on a 9 to 5 if you set appropriate expectations for your business.

As you grow, you can slowly transition into working full time on your business as your profitability and cash flow will eventually allow this, plus, you need to focus more time on your retails business and this might interfere in your daily job.

If you do get a chance to work on your business full-time, best to take it. It is the best choice to increase your chances of success as well as increase your profit potential.

Whatever time you have, focus your attention on marketing especially in the early days when you want to build momentum.

Focusing full time on your dropshipping business and a strong focus on marketing and promoting your business will help you get that average full-time income of $50,000.

In doing this, there are two things in mind:

- When your dropshipping business gets up and running, the hard part comes in maintaining your site, but this may take less time than earning that amount of money than from a 9 to 5 job. Your biggest investment would pay off in terms of scalability and efficiency that the dropshipping model offers.

- You will be creating more than just an income stream as you are building your business. You are also building yourself an asset which could be sold off in the future. You want to consider the equity value of the business that you are accruing as well as the cash flow that is generated when looking at your true returns.

Investing Money

You can create and establish a dropshipping business by investing a whole lot of money, but this is not the best advice. The most success you will achieve is when you have done the dirty work with your business.

It is extremely crucial to be the person who is deeply invested in the success of your business building it from the ground up or at least have someone who is that person. It is extremely crucial for you and your business partner to understand how your business works in each level.

While investing a lot of money in your dropshipping business is not something recommended, you still need to have some amount of cash, somewhere in the range of $1,000 for launching and operational costs for hosting fees.

Deciding on a Business Structure

Part of taking your business seriously is to set up a legitimate business entity. Here are some of the most common business structures that you can investigate for e-commerce:

- **Sole Proprietorship**

  This is a simple and straightforward business structure that you can implement in your dropshipping business. However, it also means that it offers you no protection from personal liability which means in the event your business is sued, your personal assets are also part of this equation.

  On the other hand, requirements for filing are minimal and all you must do is make sure you report on both your personal taxes as well as the earnings from your business.

- **Limited Liability Company (LLC)**

  With an LLC, your personal assets are protected because you can establish your business as a separate legal entity. This type of business structure does offer more protection than a sole proprietorship, although it is not foolproof. In this kind of business structure, you will need to adhere to certain filing requirements as well as pay certain fees.

- **C Corporation**

C Corporations, which when set up properly, offers the most liability protection and most businesses set up as C Corporation. This business structure is more on the expensive side and it is also subjected to double taxation as the income does not pass to the shareholders directly.

So, which of these structures would you choose?

Most business owners will go for LLC or sole proprietorship. For dropshipping, it is recommended to go with an LLC because it offers a better trade-off regarding autonomy from personal finances and costs and liability protection.

Making Sure Your Finances are in Order

When you start out a business, do not make the mistake of blending your business finances with your personal finances. This is confusing and audit nightmare on both a personal and professional level not to mention that it will make accounting difficult as well.

Keeping your business and personal finances separate is one of the best advice you can use no matter what kind of business you are in, dropshipping or brick-and-mortar. Opening new accounts under your business's registered name is a great way to start.

Here are the bank accounts you need to open:

- **Business Checking Account**

All your business finances need to go be run through using one main checking account. All your business revenue must be deposited into this account and any expense for your business must be withdrawn from it. This would make things easier for you, the business owner as well for your accountant.

- **PayPal Account**

PayPal accounts are great to have in your e-commerce site especially if you plan to accept payments via PayPal. For this, you will also want a business account tied to your e-commerce website.

- **Credit Card**

As credit cards are preferred payments by suppliers, credit cards are preferred methods of payment by your customers too. In that same mindset, you should also have a business credit card for the business expenses as well as for your inventory purchases for dropshipping.

There will be plenty of purchases that you will make from your suppliers and use a credit card connected to your business account enables you to gain some serious rewards. Look around for cards that give you rewards for things like travel, online transactions and certain types of merchandise that you will most likely be purchasing more often.

Collecting Sales Tax

Of course, taxes are something that you must know. You will need to collect sales tax if you fall into this category:

- The state your business is operating from collects sales tax

- An order is made by a person living in your state

Orders made by people residing in other states and even in states that have your own sales tax, you do not need to collect tax. These tax laws for online merchants are beneficial especially if you are new to dropshipping and your business is considered still small.

Local Business Licenses

Businesses need business licenses and these licenses need to be renewed on a regular basis. For dropshipping businesses, the requirements may differ, and these will likely have involved operations from home offices. When starting your dropshipping business, investigate what your local laws and regulations require, if anything.

Chapter 6 - Different Methods of Dropshipping Business

There are many ways that you can do dropshipping but, in this chapter, we will look at the most effective methods that you can try in 2018.

1 - Focus Your Time in Marketing

Many of the aspects in dropshipping retail are automated which frees up your time in focusing solely on branding and marketing your products as well as optimizing your site. Marketing is a money maker so from the logo, website look and feel to the tone of voice - you want all these things to sync in well so that you can convert your traffic to sales.

Learn to master the use of ads and optimize your website with specific keywords. These elements drive more traffic to your store and convert at least 2% of customers on a daily basis. Your objective is to get more traffic to your site so that it can generate a good percentage of sales. SEO can help drive long-term sales simply by having you rank high on search engine results.

You can do this by:

1. Creating blog content

2. Optimizing your product pages

3. Updating your pages and keep it fresh

4. Using social media to optimize being found online

2 - Create Fantastic Offers

Sales, bundles, and offers are something EVERYONE loves! It not only makes you noticeable but also increases traffic to your site! If no products on your site are for sale, customers visiting your site will lack the motivation to purchase your products. However, the right product with the right deal will more likely make them purchase on your site.

Tie offers with celebrations, holidays or even create bundle packs. When customers love a product from your site, they will likely want to purchase more of it. The hardest part is to get them to purchase - after that, it is uphill all the way!

3 - Avoid Underpricing Your Products

In dropshipping, the cost of products is usually close to wholesale price and it allows you to sell your products at market value and get a nice profit. If the cost of your product is $5 then you should be selling it for $20 so you can profit.

If your prices are fair and within market value, you should be able to gain a sizeable profit from each order made on your website.

Do not undercut your prices even when other retailers are doing so unless you are giving an offer or discount or a sale. Create strategies that will allow you to make more money overall.

4 - Choose ePacket

ePacket shipping is currently the fastest and most affordable dropshipping method. It ensures quick delivery without high costs. An ePacket shipping on average would cost you under $5 for most products so this will allow you to make a profit when you sell your product at a market value.

ePacket deliveries reach customers within 7 to 10 days from the date of purchase and are by far one of the best delivery methods for dropshippers to use.

5 - Go the Extra Mile with Customer Service

Ask anyone going to a restaurant if they would go back to a restaurant if the food was mediocre but with exceptional service. Chances are that the answer would be yes. People remember more of how you made them feel and the same applies to e-commerce as well.

Offering great customer service is one of the best ways to stand out especially if you are selling the same products as other merchants out there. Your customer service can be in the form of thank you cards included in the shipping packages or it could also be points that they have accumulated from multiple purchases which entitle them to a free gift! It can also be simple things like speedy response to their issues or complaints.

Whatever you do, make your customers feel valued and appreciated - it is because of them that you are a success.

6 - Stay Active on Your Channels

You need to put in effort on a consistent and daily basis. While you do not need to spend eight hours a day working on marketing and promoting your site, you still need to commit several hours on a daily basis to ensure that your store is updated, relevant and active.

As your business grows, so will the number of hours you need to commit to processing orders, speak with your suppliers, ensure shipping is in route and orders arrive promptly to your customers.

You will also need to ensure that your marketing efforts are in line with your products and social media is one of the best ways to stay current and relevant, ensuring that you appear at least once a day in the minds of your customers.

7 - Start With at Least 30 Items on Your Site

Don't make the mistake of importing hundreds of items to your site. While it can be exciting, the problem is that adding too many products too soon may be deadly to your site. For each product you add to your site, you need to have a few quality images, product descriptions, and keywords. Doing all of this in a short span of time can be time-consuming and exhausting, especially if you are still stuck in your day job.

Adding the product incrementally, starting with 30 would be best as you can write quality descriptions and maintain focus to start your sales and understand how your audience reacts on your site. You need to get one great product to land a sale and not 100 products. Stay focused and start small, building your way up.

8 - Monitor Your Competition

As always, you need to keep your friends close and your enemies closer. Monitor your competition's social media and their websites regularly. Like their page and you'll also receive updates on their products and the promotions they have.

By paying attention to what they do, you'll also have a better idea on how to sell your products on your store. Do not rip-off content but use it as inspiration to understand what makes or breaks attention. This not only helps bring in the audience to your site, but it also helps you make you do better in marketing your own products.

Chapter 7 - Common Dropshipping Mistakes to Avoid

By now, it should seem like dropshipping is a straightforward retail business and any person would jump at the opportunity to start. The advantages are immense and one of the biggest pull factors is the costs involved to start a dropshipping business - next to nothing.

Despite the pretty straightforward plan, you will need to understand and know what your responsibilities are as well as the mistakes that you might end up getting into. In this chapter, we will look into common mistakes retailers often make in dropshipping so you can avoid them.

1 - Worrying About Shipping Costs

Although shipping costs can be a pain, this isn't productive to worry. Your priorities need to be strategically aligned to increase sales and depending on where your orders come from, your shipping costs will be in a different range.

So, in the spirit of increasing your profits, a good thing to start with is setting a flat shipping rate which will reduce this worry for you. It is straightforward and easy for your customers and it will be easier for you.

2 - Relying Too Much on Vendors

Putting your trust in your vendor can be a forum for plenty of problems ahead. Having one vendor, for example, can mean that they may raise prices for you, go out of business, or the items run out which means you may also go out of business. What would you do then?

Having a backup supplier is what you should do. When doing business in dropshipping, it is always good to write a contract with your vendors to ensure that both of you know each other's end of the bargain.

3 - Expecting Easy Money

As we already know, dropshipping does provide a good level of convenience that does make your job a simpler one. Despite that, you need to be aware of the competition ahead of you and how important it is to market your product. This needs research as well as a unique approach that makes your product stand out amongst the masses. Don't expect money to roll in without putting in the work and time needed to see your product and your site lift out.

4 - Making Order Information Difficult to Access

Make things easy and clear for your customers and this also means providing the estimated shipping dates, so your customers know what to expect.

Keeping your customers informed of the product they are buying, the way they make payments, the information they are keying into your site as well as how long they will need to wait until their items arrive are all the things you need to put in black and white. Not only will this help you troubleshoot problems, but your customers will be happy with the information they can access.

5 - Not Enough Brand Display

The one major drawback of dropshipping is that it can be hard to ensure that your brand is prominent to your customers not only in the look and feel but also the entire customer experience. You don't want your customers to forget you, you need to work extra hard to insert your brand as much as possible in every corner you can.

One of the best things you can do is to ensure you develop a good working relationship with your supplier and get them to insert custom packaging for you to remind them of you and show them you care about their experience at the same time.

6 - Botching Order Changes and Cancellations

Your online customers change their minds faster than the ones who shop at regular stores. This is bound to happen and for this, you need a backup plan as well. You want to ensure that your customer is efficiently and accurately refunded.

Some vendors will immediately go ahead and make the order and you'll end up with a negative review on your site. To avoid this, speak to your vendor first before confirming things with your customer. While your customers wait for confirmation, let them know you have received their request and are working on making the necessary refunds or changes.

7 - Mishandling Damaged or Lost Items — plus Other Shipping Issues

The minute a customer experiences problem with their order, their frustrations are immediately directed at you. When this happens, you need to be prepared to offer your customers an easy and quick solution. Be sure that you create a process for managing and handling problematic orders, so you can keep your customers happy.

8 - Return Complications

Setting up a system for returns will be beneficial not only for your sanity but also to reduce the time your customers need to wait for a result. Organized and systematic approaches to problems not only keep your customers happy but it also shows you are professional.

Chapter 8 - Tips and Tricks in Dropshipping

Tips and tricks are always great for anything new that you are learning - it makes us able to accomplish things better, more efficiently, in less time and achieve better results.

Here are eight tips to master your online dropshipping business:

1 - Keep Your Eye on the Ball

Your main goal is to create profits, so that should be your focus. Do not get carried away by flashy graphics and so called 'must-haves' for your website or even long content that apparently 'speaks' to your audience. You do not want to lengthen the time it takes for your customers to decide to purchase your product.

The idea is to get them to your site, browse for what they want, click on the product, read a short description and buy it. Keep things moving forward and avoid anything that detracts you from this mission.

2 - Think Like a Customer

One of the reasons why you need to stick to a niche that you know and one that you are passionate about is, so you understand customer pain points.

What do you look for when you are on someone's website? What do you expect to find there? What kind of buying process makes you feel you purchase things fast? What makes you like the website you usually purchase from?

Knowing the pain points yourself makes you understand what your customers want and how your product can help them accomplish their needs.

3 - SEO Your Site

Part of your marketing should also be SEO. SEO is not dead so long as keywords are still used to search for anything and everything on the internet. You need to use SEO wisely, not only on your website but also on your social media which is from content, titles, tags, image tags, descriptions- the whole nine yards. You will be found much easier through specific keywords.

4 - Product Reviews

The best way for any customer to know that the products they are purchasing are value for money is by reading reviews. Customers will click on products that have higher ratings and the likelihood of them purchasing it is if it has good and high reviews.

DO NOT cheat on your reviews. If you have a product that always gets bad reviews - trash it. When you do, let your customers know that you are discontinuing it because this will help increase their confidence in your site. The fact that you have heard them, and you are doing something about it increases brand trust.

5 - Mix Your Marketing

There are many ways to reach your customers depending on who they are and what they do. For most dropshipping marketing methods, social media marketing and email marketing is the way to go. But you should not rely on it entirely.

It is also good to meet with your customers and see who they are. Host product giveaways, hold online workshops or seminars, have an online meet-and-greet, feature your customers using your product or give them a shout out!

6 - Make Your Logistics Work Well

Have strong and clear agreements on any potential logistical issues that you may encounter in your dropshipping business. Outline these in your contract and have this on your website. Inform customers what to do if they have returned.

Outline this with your supplier as well and establish standard operating procedures for returns, damaged items and so on. Outline what the shipping costs are as well between yourself and the supplier and what is the expected delivery date for your items between supplier and customer.

7 - Establish Your Relationship with Your Supplier

Establishing and maintaining close relationships with your suppliers ensures that you can also extend the benefits to your customers.

When you supplier trusts you, there will be many things that you can get done such as offer personalized packaging to your customers, ensuring speedy shipping and having reduced time in managing any issues you must deal with if there are delays. Collaboration is based on trust and the quicker you establish trust, the better.

8 - Communicate Your Product Strategy

Strong product descriptions ensure higher success rates of purchasing. This information is critical to your customer - they want to know what they are buying and the better you describe your product, the faster it would be for your customers to make a purchasing decision.

Do not give long and vague descriptions and do not put in duplicate content. Duplicate content will be penalized by search engines.

Conclusion

If you ever dreamt of running your own business with an easy and simple retail model, dropshipping is for you and where you start. Don't worry about failing - dropshipping involves minimal startup costs and honestly, there is no failure unless you do not put in the necessary time and effort it takes to get the business off the ground.

Many dropship retailers go into the business without any clue except to succeed in the e-commerce world. By reading this guide, you are more equipped than any of the new entrepreneurs because you have made this step to do your research, learn and find out what the fundamentals of dropshipping. You are already 80% equipped and ready to go!

Go out there and create a business with value and you will be on your way to a successful business. Don't think about making money fast but have the desire to create value and change the lives of the people that purchase your product.

Final Words

I would like to thank you for purchasing my book and I hope I have been able to help you and educate you on something new.

If you have enjoyed this book and would like to share your positive thoughts, could you please take 30 seconds of your time to go back and give me a review on my Amazon book page!

I greatly appreciate seeing these reviews because it helps me share my hard work!

Again, thank you and I wish you all the best!

Disclaimer

I have created this book with the purpose to provide information on dropshipping.

It is sold with the understanding that the author and publisher are not engaged in any sort of professional services or legal advice.

Every effort has been made to ensure this book is complete and without error, however, it's possible that there may be errors, whether in content or other.

Therefore, do not consider this to be anything more than a guide and a book created for entertainment purposes.

The author and publisher are not liable or responsible for any damages or losses incurred by any person, which has allegedly been caused directly or indirectly by the information within this book.

If you do not agree with the above information, simply contact the author for a full refund.